We Are NOT in This Together

The Privileges of Political Life

Billy J Riggs

ISBN: 9798230287001

First printing 2024

WE ARE NOT IN THIE TOGETHER

First edition. November 23, 2024.

ISBN: 979-8230287001

Written by Bill Riggs.

CHAPTER 1

Introduction

In recent years, the phrase "we're in this together" has emerged as a prominent slogan, frequently used by politicians, corporate leaders, and members of the World Economic Forum (WEF) to emphasize unity and collective action in the face of global challenges. This phrase, though seemingly simple, carries significant weight in political and social discourse, especially in times of crisis, such as the COVID-19 pandemic and the ongoing efforts to address climate change, economic inequality, and geopolitical instability.

The widespread adoption of this slogan by global leaders signals an attempt to foster a sense of shared responsibility and solidarity among nations, communities, and individuals. It suggests that the solutions to the world's most pressing problems require collaborative efforts that transcend national borders, social classes, and individual interests. The World Economic Forum, in particular, has championed this message as part of its broader agenda of "stakeholder capitalism" and global governance, which emphasizes that businesses, governments, and civil society must work together to achieve sustainable development and equitable economic growth.

While the phrase often resonates as a call for unity, it has also sparked criticism and skepticism. Many view it as an empty platitude, pointing out that the burden of crises like economic downturns, pandemics, and climate change disproportionately affects the poor and vulnerable, while elites and powerful institutions face fewer consequences. As a result, "we're in this together" has come to symbolize both the hope for collective progress and the growing distrust between citizens and global leaders. Understanding the origins and use of this phrase in modern discourse requires unpacking its political and social implications. It reflects both an idealistic vision of a united global community and the complex realities of power, privilege, and inequality that complicate the notion of shared sacrifice.

A 2014 study titled "Testing Theories of American Politics: Elites, Interest Groups, and Average Citizens," conducted by political scientists Martin Gilens of Princeton University and Benjamin I. Page of Northwestern University, is one of the most significant empirical analyses on the nature of political power and influence in the United States. The study sought to determine who truly holds sway over U.S. public policy: the general population, economic elites, or organized interest groups. It challenged the assumption that America operates as a functioning democracy, wherein government policies reflect the will of the average citizen, and instead provided evidence that the policy-making process is heavily dominated by economic elites and interest groups.

Gilens and Page analyzed nearly 1,800 policy issues over a period of 20 years, examining how the preferences of four key groups—average citizens, economic elites, mass-based interest groups, and business-oriented interest groups—influenced U.S. policy outcomes. Their findings were stark and concerning for proponents of democratic governance. The study concluded that:

Economic elites and organized business interest groups have a substantial, independent impact on U.S. government policy, whereas the preferences of average citizens have little to no independent influence. Average citizens' preferences are almost completely ignored unless they happen to align with those of economic elites or organized interest groups. Mass-based interest groups (such as labor unions or large advocacy organizations) had some impact, but their influence was far less significant compared to business-oriented interest groups.

This evidence strongly suggested that, in practice, the United States operates more as an oligarchy or plutocracy, where a small group of elites control policy outcomes, rather than a true democracy where all citizens have equal influence on governmental decisions.

The study aimed to test four theoretical perspectives on how American politics functions:

Majoritarian Electoral Democracy: This theory posits that the U.S. operates as a democracy in which policy outcomes reflect the preferences of the majority of voters. In this model, elected officials are responsive to the average citizen's policy preferences because they rely on their votes to stay in office.

Economic Elite Domination: This theory suggests that policy outcomes are shaped by the preferences of wealthy individuals and large corporations. Economic elites, due to their resources and influence, are able to steer government policy to align with their interests.

Majoritarian Pluralism: This model envisions that politics is driven by the competition between organized interest groups that represent various segments of society. Ideally, these groups counterbalance each other, leading to policy outcomes that reflect the interests of the broader population.

Biased Pluralism: This theory suggests that interest group competition is skewed in favor of business-oriented and wealthy groups. The idea here is that certain powerful interest groups—particularly those representing corporations or industries—hold disproportionate influence, leading to policy outcomes that primarily benefit elites.

Gilens and Page's findings overwhelmingly supported the Economic Elite Domination and Biased Pluralism theories. Policies, they found, were rarely in line with the preferences of the average citizen, unless those preferences happened to coincide with those of the wealthy or well-organized business groups. The idea of majoritarian democracy, where citizens' views are reflected in policy decisions, was found to be largely a myth.

A clear illustration of this dynamic can be seen in the aftermath of the 2008 financial crisis. The crisis, which resulted from risky behavior by financial institutions, led to widespread economic devastation for millions of average Americans. Many lost their homes, jobs, and savings due to the collapse of the housing market and subsequent recession.

Following the crisis, there was significant public outcry for stronger financial regulations to prevent a similar meltdown in the future. Polls at the time showed that the majority of average citizens favored stringent regulation of the financial sector. However, despite the broad public support for tough reforms, the resulting Dodd-Frank Wall Street Reform and Consumer Protection Act was relatively moderate and left many loopholes for financial institutions.

One of the reasons for this outcome, as Gilens and Page's findings would suggest, was the outsized influence of economic elites and business-oriented interest groups. Financial institutions, which have significant resources, invest heavily in lobbying efforts and campaign contributions to shape the reform legislation in their favor. In contrast, the preferences of the average citizen, who desired more aggressive reform, were largely ignored in the final policy outcome.

For instance, while Dodd-Frank introduced some new regulations, such as the creation of the Consumer Financial Protection Bureau (CFPB), it did not break up the largest financial institutions or implement the most aggressive forms of regulation that many Americans had hoped for. Wall Street banks and financial industry groups were able to significantly water down key provisions of the legislation, ensuring that their interests were protected, despite public opposition.

This example illustrates the core finding of Gilens and Page's study, that the preferences of elites and interest groups are much more influential in shaping policy than those of average citizens. Even in the wake of a catastrophic event like the 2008 financial crisis, where the public's demand for reform was clear, the resulting policies largely reflected the interests of the powerful financial industry rather than the desires of the majority of Americans.

The implications of Gilens and Page's study are profound. Their findings suggest that American democracy is deeply flawed in terms of representing the interests of its citizens. While elections may provide the appearance of democracy, the reality is that powerful elites and interest groups have an outsized influence on policy decisions. This raises critical questions about the nature of political power in the U.S. and the effectiveness of democratic governance.

Since average citizens have little influence over the policies that shape their lives, it has led to a sense of disenfranchisement and mistrust in the political system. The study highlights how the gap between the wealthy and the rest of society is not just economic, but also political, with the wealthy and business elites able to translate their economic power into political influence, reinforcing and perpetuating inequality.

The study fundamentally challenges the notion that the United States is a functioning democracy in which the will of the people is reflected in policy outcomes. Instead, the findings suggest that the policy-making process is dominated by economic elites and interest groups, with the preferences of average citizens often ignored. Through examples like the aftermath of the 2008 financial crisis, the study illustrates how powerful interest groups and wealthy individuals are able to shape government policies to align with their interests, leaving the average citizen with little real influence. This calls into question the core principles of representative democracy and highlights the need for systemic reforms to make the political process more equitable and responsive to the needs of all citizens, not just the wealthy few.

CHAPTER 2

The Origins of Similar Ideologies

In many ways, the ideology that places the burden of crises like economic downturns, pandemics, and climate change disproportionately on the working class and poor while allowing elites and powerful institutions to evade accountability mirrors some of the critiques made by Marxist-Leninist, Socialist, and Communist ideologies. Throughout history, periods of economic, environmental, and social crises have often disproportionately impacted the middle class and the poor, while elites and powerful institutions have found ways to shield themselves from the most severe consequences. This imbalance is not new but rooted in long-standing ideologies and political systems that reinforce wealth concentration and limit accountability for those at the top.

In practice, Marxist-Leninist, Socialist, and Communist states have always disproportionately burdened the working class. While these systems were designed, in theory, to abolish class distinctions and create a classless society, in reality, many of them simply replaced the capitalist elite with a new ruling class, the political elite or party officials. In Marxist-Leninist regimes like the Soviet Union or Maoist China, the political leadership justified its rule by claiming to act in the interests of the working class. However, during periods of economic depression, economic failure, or political crisis, it was often the ordinary citizens and workers who suffered most, while the political elites enjoyed a degree of protection and privilege.

One of the most tragic examples of this was the Holodomor in Ukraine in the early 1930s. Under Joseph Stalin's rule, the Soviet Union sought to rapidly industrialize through forced collectivization, which led to mass starvation as agricultural output plummeted. While millions of peasants and workers died or were left to starve, the Soviet leadership continued to control resources, ration food selectively, and maintain a comfortable standard of living. The same ruling class that claimed to represent the proletariat ultimately placed the burden of the crisis on the very people they purported to empower.

Similarly, the Great Chinese Famine during Mao Zedong's "Great Leap Forward" (1958-1962) saw millions of Chinese peasants starve as the government pushed unrealistic industrial and agricultural quotas. While rural farmers suffered massive losses, Communist Party officials and the elite were insulated from the most severe consequences, continuing to live relatively comfortably in urban centers. These examples show how crises in Marxist-Leninist systems also led to disproportionate suffering for the working class, echoing some of the same dynamics seen in various recent crises.

In both Marxist-Leninist and capitalist systems, political and economic elites tend to consolidate power and evade responsibility during times of crisis. In capitalist systems, it is the financial elite, large corporations, and wealthy individuals who can avoid accountability. As in Marxist-Leninist systems, the ruling party or political elite, despite parroting the benefits of a theoretical classless society, effectively function as the bourgeoisie in a Marxist state, exploiting the working class and benefiting from the state's power while avoiding the consequences of economic and social failures.

The Newest Burden on the Working Class

Climate change, much like economic downturns or pandemics, represents another area where the working class and poor disproportionately suffer, while elites face fewer consequences. Whether in capitalist or socialist systems, those with power and resources tend to be more insulated from the environmental impacts of climate change.

In capitalist societies, wealthy individuals and corporations can afford to mitigate the effects of climate change, whether by relocating to safer areas, investing in cleaner technologies, or lobbying governments to delay strict environmental regulations. Meanwhile, poor communities, particularly those in developing countries or coastal regions, are more vulnerable to extreme weather events, rising sea levels, and resource scarcity. These communities often lack the political influence to advocate for environmental justice or to hold polluters accountable.

In socialist systems, the same dynamic can occur when the state prioritizes industrial production or economic growth over environmental concerns. For example, during the Soviet era, the government's focus on heavy industry and rapid modernization led to severe environmental degradation, which disproportionately affected rural and working-class citizens. The infamous Chernobyl disaster in 1986 is a prime example of how the Soviet leadership shielded itself from accountability, while ordinary citizens were left to suffer the consequences of radiation exposure, displacement, and environmental contamination.

In both capitalist and Marxist-Leninist systems, the working class and poor consistently bear the heaviest burden during crises, while elites manage to evade accountability and protect their wealth and privileges. Whether in capitalist societies where financial institutions receive bailouts while ordinary people lose their jobs, or in Marxist-Leninist states where political elites enjoy privileges while the working class faces financial ruin, the common thread is that those with power and resources often shift the costs of crises onto the most vulnerable. This pattern underscores the persistence of class divisions and unequal accountability, regardless of the ideological system in place.

Not a New Phenomenon

The practice of placing the heaviest burdens of crises on the lower classes dates back to feudal societies, where the aristocracy maintained control over land, wealth, and political power. While the mechanisms in capitalist societies differ from those in Marxist-Leninist states, the end result, where the burden of economic or social crises falls heavily on the working class, shares important similarities. Historically, during times of economic depression, war, or disease, it was the peasants and laborers who bore the brunt of suffering, while lords and monarchs preserved their wealth and status. In exchange for protection or governance, the lower classes were expected to pay taxes or provide labor, with little regard for their ability to sustain themselves during hard times.

This dynamic persisted into the Industrial Revolution, which saw the rise of capitalism and a new elite class of industrialists and financiers. As factories and large corporations became the economic engines of society, laborers faced poor working conditions, low wages, and minimal social safety nets. Meanwhile, the owners of capital amassed tremendous wealth, often with minimal government intervention. When economic downturns, such as the Panic of 1873 or the Great Depression of the 1930s, occurred, it was the working and middle classes that faced unemployment, poverty, and loss of livelihood. Wealthy industrialists, bankers, and corporate elites often survived these crises through government bailouts, favorable economic policies, or control of capital, leaving the less affluent to struggle.

Examples of Disproportionate Burden

The Great Depression of the 1930s exemplifies how economic crises place unequal burdens on society. Millions of Americans lost their jobs, homes, and savings during this period, and many families faced extreme poverty. The working class, small business owners, and farmers were hit the hardest. Meanwhile, large corporations and banks, many of which played a role in creating the financial bubble that led to the stock market crash of 1929, lobbied for government intervention and, in many cases, received direct assistance.

For example, many banks received federal aid through programs like the Reconstruction Finance Corporation, created to stabilize key industries. Though this saved certain institutions from collapse, it did not address the immediate needs of unemployed workers or impoverished families. As a result, large businesses and financial institutions rebounded while the average citizen struggled to survive, a trend that would be repeated in future economic crises.

In the latter half of the 20th century, the rise of neoliberal economic policies, pioneered by leaders like Ronald Reagan in the U.S. and Margaret Thatcher in the U.K., further entrenched these dynamics. Neoliberalism emphasized deregulation, privatization, and tax cuts for the wealthy, under the assumption that a free market would drive economic growth that would ultimately benefit all. In practice, however, these policies often exacerbated income inequality, as corporations and wealthy individuals accrued more power and wealth while social safety nets for the poor and middle class were dismantled.

An example of this occurred during the 2008 Global Financial Crisis, which was triggered by reckless behavior within the financial sector, the response from governments around the world disproportionately favored banks and large corporations. Governments, particularly in the U.S., implemented massive bailouts for Wall Street institutions through programs like the Troubled Asset Relief Program (TARP), injecting trillions of dollars into financial institutions to stabilize the economy.

While this action arguably prevented an even greater economic collapse, the middle class and working poor, those who lost homes, jobs, and retirement savings, saw little direct relief. Millions of families faced foreclosure, unemployment skyrocketed, and entire communities were devastated. Meanwhile, banks and corporations recovered swiftly, with executives receiving bonuses and the stock market rebounding far more quickly than wages or employment rates.

In contrast, policies that cut public spending in an effort to reduce national deficits, were frequently applied to social programs that benefited the poor and middle class. Governments, particularly in Europe, cut funding for healthcare, education, and welfare programs, further burdening those already struggling in the aftermath of the crisis.

A More Recent Example

The COVID-19 pandemic of 2020 further revealed the disparity in how crises affect different social classes. While governments implemented stimulus packages and relief programs, the wealthiest individuals and institutions often emerged even more prosperous, while working-class individuals and small business owners faced devastating economic consequences.

As governments worldwide enforced lockdowns to control the spread of the virus, the middle class and poor, many of whom worked in service industries, manufacturing, and healthcare, were often unable to work from home. Millions of workers in industries like hospitality, retail, and transportation lost their jobs or had their hours reduced. In contrast, many white-collar professionals in industries like tech or finance were able to work remotely, preserving their income.

Large corporations, particularly in the tech sector, flourished during the pandemic. Companies like Amazon, Apple, and Google saw their profits soar as consumers increasingly relied on digital services, online shopping, and remote work solutions. Meanwhile, small businesses faced significant challenges. Many small restaurant owners, retail stores, and service providers went bankrupt or closed permanently due to restrictions, while large corporations had the resources to survive or even expand during the crisis. For example, Amazon saw record profits during the pandemic, as consumers turned to online shopping while small brick-and-mortar stores shuttered.

Government relief efforts, while substantial, also favored larger institutions. In the U.S., the Paycheck Protection Program (PPP) was designed to help small businesses keep employees on the payroll during the pandemic. However, large corporations and well-connected businesses with access to financial resources often navigated the system more effectively, securing larger portions of the available funds. Many truly small businesses, particularly minority-owned and local enterprises, struggled to access these funds and suffered disproportionate losses.

At the same time, policy solutions to climate change can place further strain on lower-income individuals. Carbon taxes, for instance, are often designed to reduce emissions by making it more expensive to use fossil fuels. However, these taxes can disproportionately impact poorer households, who spend a larger share of their income on energy and transportation. In many cases, wealthier individuals and corporations have the resources to invest in cleaner technologies, while low-income populations bear the brunt of the costs associated with the transition to a greener economy.

Avoidance of Accountability by Elites

The avoidance of accountability by elites during these crises is often facilitated by their political influence, wealth, and ability to shape policy outcomes. In many cases, powerful institutions are able to mitigate the damage they cause through lobbying, legal protections, or favorable regulations. They also have access to teams of lawyers, public relations experts, and crisis management consultants that can protect their reputations and financial interests.

For example, during the 2008 financial crisis, many of the key figures in the banking sector who were responsible for risky practices that contributed to the economic collapse faced few personal consequences. While millions of Americans lost their homes, the executives of major financial institutions largely avoided criminal charges, and many even received large bonuses after their companies were bailed out. This avoidance of accountability reflects a broader trend in which elites and powerful institutions are often able to sidestep the legal and financial consequences of their actions, while ordinary citizens bear the costs.

The practice of placing the burden of crises on the middle class and the poor while elites avoid accountability is rooted in historical economic and political ideologies that prioritize the protection of wealth and power. From feudal systems to modern neoliberal capitalism, the patterns remain consistent: in times of crisis, those with political and economic influence use their power to shield themselves from the fallout, while the vulnerable pay the price. As seen in the Great Depression, the 2008 financial crisis, the COVID-19 pandemic, and the ongoing climate crisis, the disparity between how different social classes experience and recover from crises highlights the deep inequalities that persist in modern society. We are NOT in this together.

CHAPTER 3

A Tale of Two Budgets

Imagine two organizations, each with a similar number of employees, let's say 15 people. One is a congressional office, tasked with serving the constituents of a U.S. Representative. The other is a private company, a small to mid-sized business focused on producing and selling a product or service. While both have the same number of people on their payroll, their operating budgets, priorities, and constraints are worlds apart.

A congressional office receives its operating budget from the U.S. House of Representatives or the Senate, which is determined by a fixed formula and is not subject to the fluctuations of market demand or business cycles. For example, each office in the House of Representatives has an annual budget known as the Members' Representational Allowance (MRA), which averages around $1.5 to $2 million, depending on the district's distance from Washington D.C., the number of constituents, and other factors. The budget is used to cover salaries, office supplies, travel, and other expenses necessary for the office's functioning.

Unlike in a private company, this budget is not influenced by profits or revenues. It is funded entirely by taxpayer dollars. The office must operate within its allocated budget, and any unused funds typically do not roll over to the next year but are returned to the Treasury. Congressional staff salaries are generally lower compared to their private-sector counterparts, and the budget must also accommodate district office expenses, constituent services, and legislative functions. The office must balance several priorities: maintaining constituent services, managing legislative responsibilities, communicating with voters, and complying with legal and ethical guidelines. There is little flexibility for bonuses, raises, or performance incentives.

Now consider a private company with the same number of employees. Unlike the congressional office, its budget is inherently internally generated and directly tied to its revenue and market performance. The company may allocate funds for salaries, marketing, research and development, production costs, and other operating expenses. The total budget might range significantly depending on the company's size, industry, and growth stage.

A private company's budget is built to adapt. If revenues increase, the company might invest more in hiring, expanding operations, or launching new products. Conversely, if revenues decline or taxes increase, the company may cut costs, lay off employees, or pivot to new markets. The emphasis is on profitability and efficiency, and every dollar spent is typically weighed against its potential return on investment. In a private company, unlike taxpayer funded congressional budgets, there is intense pressure from stakeholders, investors, or owners to deliver financial results.

Thus, while both entities may employ the same number of people, their financial landscapes are funded and shaped by fundamentally different forces, one by the requirements of governance and public tax dollars, and the other by the imperatives of the marketplace. We are NOT in this together.

Expanding the Comparison

Let's delve deeper into how the operating budgets of a congressional office and a private company are funded and explore whether their revenue is tied to performance or productivity.

A congressional office's budget comes from a single, predictable source: the federal government. Specifically, it is funded through taxpayer dollars appropriated by Congress itself as part of the federal budget process. Each congressional office receives an annual allocation known as the Members' Representational Allowance (MRA) in the

House of Representatives or an equivalent allowance in the Senate. These funds are allocated based on a formula that accounts for the number of constituents in the district, the cost of office space and operations in the area, and the distance from Washington, D.C.

The congressional office's funding comes from federal tax revenues collected from individuals, businesses, and other entities across the United States. This money is part of a larger pool that Congress allocates for various governmental functions, including defense, healthcare, education, and other public services. The portion allocated to congressional offices is relatively small but consistent, given the importance of maintaining a functional legislative branch.

Unlike a private company, a congressional office's funding is not tied to its performance or productivity. Each office receives its budget regardless of how well it serves its constituents, how many bills it sponsors, or how effectively it operates. There is no direct financial incentive for a congressional office to be more efficient or productive since its budget remains the same regardless of its output. However, the performance of a congressional office can impact the re-election prospects of the Member of Congress. If constituents feel neglected or believe their needs are not being met, they might choose not to re-elect their representative.

In contrast, a private company's budget, on the other hand, is inherently dynamic and directly tied to its ability to generate revenue in the marketplace. This revenue can come from several sources, including sales of products or services, investments, loans, or other income streams. The operating budget of a private company is funded primarily by the money it earns from its customers. The primary source of revenue for a private company is its sales, whether it's selling goods, services, or a combination of both. Unlike a congressional office that relies on a pre-allocated budget, a private company's revenue is tied to consumer demand and market conditions. If the company sells more products or services, its revenue increases; if sales decline, so does the budget.

Unlike a congressional office, a private company's revenue is highly dependent on its performance and productivity. For a private business, growth in revenue typically requires effective marketing, quality products or services, competitive pricing, efficient operations, and strong customer relationships. If the company performs poorly, its revenue will suffer, potentially leading to budget cuts, layoffs, or even bankruptcy. Moreover, in many private companies, employee compensation, bonuses, and promotions are directly tied to performance metrics such as sales targets, customer satisfaction ratings, or productivity benchmarks. This creates a strong incentive for employees to perform well, innovate, and contribute to the company's overall success.

A congressional office has a guaranteed budget funded by taxpayer dollars and allocated based on a set formula, regardless of the office's effectiveness or efficiency. A private company must earn its income through sales, investments, or other revenue-generating activities. Its budget is fluid and fluctuates with market performance, consumer demand. In a congressional office, the budget is not directly tied to measurable outcomes or performance metrics. While poor performance could indirectly impact the officeholder's political career, it does not affect the immediate funding of the office. Conversely, for a private company, revenue and budget are directly tied to performance and productivity. The company's success or failure in generating income drives its ability to fund operations, expand, compensate employees, and pay the taxes levied by local, state, and the federal government to support their budgets.

While both a congressional office and a private company may employ the same number of people, their funding models are fundamentally different. The congressional office operates with a fixed budget funded by private companies and individual taxpayers and is insulated from direct market forces. A private company's budget reflects its ability to compete, innovate, and meet consumer needs. One is centered on alleged public service with a stable but inflexible budget; the other is driven by market success, with a budget that is as dynamic as the economy it operates within.

The Consequences of Fiscal Mismanagement

Imagine two parallel worlds. In one, a congressional office handles its budget poorly, failing to prioritize spending, overestimating costs, or making imprudent decisions. In the other, a private company stumbles into financial mismanagement, overspending on unnecessary expenses, ignoring market signals, or making bad investments. While both scenarios involve poor financial stewardship, the consequences for each organization differ greatly in nature, impact, and scope.

A congressional office operates within a strictly allocated budget, funded entirely by taxpayer dollars. When such an office engages in fiscal mismanagement, spending funds unwisely, overspending in some areas while neglecting others, or failing to adhere to the strict rules governing its expenditures, the consequences, while not always immediately catastrophic, can be significant and felt directly by the taxpayer.

The primary consequence of mismanaging a congressional office budget is a loss of public trust. Its budget is fixed for the year, and there is no option to request additional funding mid-year if funds are exhausted. Mismanagement of funds could mean the office runs out of money before the fiscal year ends, forcing staff layoffs, cutting services, or even temporarily shutting down the office until new funds are allocated. Since the office is funded by taxpayer dollars, any perception that these funds are being wasted or misused can lead to public outrage, negative media coverage, and political fallout. Constituents expect their representatives to be good stewards of public resources, and any breach of that expectation can damage the officeholder's reputation and career. In extreme cases, allegations of financial mismanagement can trigger investigations by the House Ethics Committee or other oversight bodies, potentially leading to fines, censures, or even removal from office.

For the Member of Congress, poor financial management might become a key issue in the next election campaign, with opponents using it to attack the member's competence and integrity. Mismanagement could lead to the loss of re-election and the end of a political career, especially in closely contested districts where every misstep is magnified. And that's about the extent of their accountability.

In contrast, fiscal mismanagement in a private company has an entirely different set of consequences, largely dictated by market forces. Private companies operate in a competitive environment where survival depends on profitability, efficiency, and the ability to adapt to changing conditions. The most immediate consequence of fiscal mismanagement in a private company is a direct hit to the company's financial health. Overspending, poor investment choices, or failure to control costs can quickly deplete cash reserves, increase debt, and lead to liquidity problems. Unlike a congressional office with a guaranteed budget, a private company relies on continuous revenue generation to fund its operations. Financial mismanagement can disrupt this balance, leading to cash flow shortages and an inability to pay suppliers, creditors, or even employees.

Mismanagement can erode a company's competitive position in the market. For example, if the company over-invests in a failed product line or spends excessively on unnecessary overhead while neglecting core competencies, it risks losing market share to more agile and efficient competitors. In a highly competitive market, such missteps can quickly lead to a downward spiral of declining sales, shrinking profit margins, a tarnished brand reputation, and often bankruptcy.

In extreme cases, fiscal mismanagement can lead to bankruptcy or business closure. If a company cannot recover from poor financial decisions, cannot secure additional financing, or fails to regain profitability, it may have to file for bankruptcy protection. This can result in layoffs, liquidation of assets, loss of investor confidence, and potential closure of the business. For small businesses or startups, where financial margins are often thin, a few months of poor management can spell the end of the company.

Private companies are accountable not only to customers but also to a range of stakeholders, including investors, creditors, employees, and the government. Fiscal mismanagement can lead to lawsuits from shareholders, demands for leadership changes, and pressure from creditors. Investors might sell their shares, causing a drop in stock price, while lenders might demand repayment, further straining the company's finances. Employees may face layoffs, pay cuts, or the loss of benefits as the company struggles to right itself.

Beyond immediate financial harm, fiscal mismanagement can have lasting effects on a company's strategic direction. Poor financial decisions can stifle innovation, reduce the company's ability to invest in new opportunities, or force it to abandon strategic initiatives. Over time, this can lead to a loss of industry relevance and make it harder for the company to attract top talent. In this respect, it's similar to government.

For a congressional office, fiscal mismanagement primarily affects its ability to serve constituents effectively and uphold public trust. But there is no threat to survival. For a private company, mismanagement affects its profitability, market position, and ultimately its very existence.

Consequences of Poor Decisions

When lawmakers and private citizens make poor life or business decisions that result in major financial losses, the consequences they face are markedly different. The distinction is largely due to the nature of their employment, the public scrutiny on lawmakers, and the legal frameworks governing both groups. Lawmakers, because of their public office, operate under different rules and expectations than private citizens who work in the corporate or business world. This divergence is especially apparent in areas such as continued employment, legal repercussions, and public accountability.

One of the starkest differences between lawmakers and private citizens lies in how poor financial decisions impact their continued employment. While both groups can suffer professional damage from financial mismanagement, lawmakers are generally more insulated from the immediate consequences due to the structure of political office and the process for removing elected officials. Lawmakers who make poor decisions, whether personal or financial, often retain their positions unless their actions are particularly egregious and lead to public outrage or legal intervention. This protection comes from the fact that lawmakers are elected officials, not employees in the traditional sense, and their continued employment depends on the electorate or internal processes like impeachment, recall, or censure.

A lawmaker might be involved in a personal financial scandal, such as excessive personal spending or questionable financial investments that lead to bankruptcy. While this could hurt their public image, it may not directly result in job loss unless it leads to criminal charges or an official ethics investigation. A congressperson involved in a bad investment may face public criticism and may even be investigated by an ethics committee, but they could continue to serve out their term at full pay and benefits unless voters remove them in the next election or they resign under pressure.

In many cases, lawmakers can recover from financial mismanagement if they maintain political support. For example, in cases where politicians are involved in tax evasion or mismanaging public funds, they might face ethics investigations or fines, but unless they are convicted of a crime or censured by their governing body, they might remain in office. In extreme cases, voters might continue to support the lawmaker, if they believe the financial mismanagement does not affect their ability to represent their constituents.

Even when poor financial decisions lead to scandals, lawmakers can survive if they maintain political backing. High-profile examples include politicians involved in financial impropriety who nevertheless win re-election because their political base remains loyal or sees the issue as secondary to the lawmaker's overall performance. For instance, some members of Congress have faced accusations of misusing campaign funds or engaging in insider trading yet have continued to hold office due to a combination of political maneuvering and the slow nature of legal proceedings.

In the real world, private citizens who make poor business or financial decisions typically face more immediate and severe employment consequences. If a private citizen runs a business into the ground or is responsible for major financial losses within a company, their job security is often directly threatened. Business owners may face bankruptcy, and employees may be fired or demoted for their role in financial mismanagement.

A private citizen who owns a small business, such as a retail store or restaurant, and makes poor financial decisions, such as taking on excessive debt or mismanaging cash flow, might end up closing their business, losing their primary source of income. Additionally, if an individual is an employee in a corporate setting and is responsible for a significant financial loss due to poor decision-making, such as making a bad investment or failing to manage resources effectively, they are likely to be terminated.

In the private sector, performance is often directly tied to employment status. A business owner who faces bankruptcy due to poor financial decisions will not only lose their business but could also struggle to find new employment due to the stigma of financial failure. Similarly, a corporate executive who makes bad investment decisions that lead to major financial losses could be fired, sued by shareholders, or barred from holding executive positions in the future.

While lawmakers may be able to continue serving in office despite financial losses, private citizens are often forced to deal with the immediate fallout of personal bankruptcy or financial ruin. For example, a private citizen who files for bankruptcy might lose their home, vehicles, or personal assets. In contrast, a lawmaker facing personal financial struggles will not experience the same direct employment consequences unless they violate specific laws or ethical rules.

Breaking the Law

Both lawmakers and private citizens are subject to legal consequences when financial mismanagement rises to the level of criminal activity, but the nature of these consequences differ based on their public or private roles. Lawmakers, while not immune to the law, often face a different process for legal consequences than private citizens. If a lawmaker engages in illegal financial behavior, such as corruption, bribery, or misuse of public funds, they can be investigated and prosecuted. However, the process of holding a lawmaker accountable often involves multiple steps, including investigations by ethics committees, possible impeachment, and, ultimately, legal trials.

For example, in cases of illegal financial behavior, such as a congressperson accepting bribes or engaging in insider trading, the lawmaker could be investigated by federal agencies like the FBI or SEC. If the investigation leads to charges, the lawmaker may face criminal prosecution, but the process can take years. For instance, in high-profile corruption cases, lawmakers might be indicted for financial crimes but continue to serve until a conviction is reached. Additionally, lawmakers are often granted some level of immunity while performing their official duties, which can slow down the legal process.

While lawmakers can eventually face legal consequences, the public nature of their positions means that they often have more time and money to mitigate the damage or negotiate plea deals that might allow them to avoid the most severe penalties, such as jail time. Even in cases where lawmakers are convicted, they retain their pensions or other benefits, which private citizens typically do not enjoy.

Private citizens, especially business owners or corporate executives, are subject to more immediate legal consequences when financial mismanagement involves illegal activity. If a private citizen engages in financial fraud, tax evasion, or embezzlement, they can be sued, fined, or prosecuted without the buffer of political office. In these cases, legal consequences are often swift and decisive.

A private citizen running a small business who engages in tax fraud or embezzlement is likely to face immediate legal consequences once the wrongdoing is uncovered. This could result in heavy fines, loss of business licenses, or even prison sentences, as seen in cases where small business owners or corporate executives are found guilty of mismanaging funds or engaging in fraudulent activities. Additionally, private citizens who make poor financial decisions that harm their business often lose their entire livelihoods, as well as their ability to recover through public influence.

Private citizens are more vulnerable to civil lawsuits and personal financial ruin following financial mismanagement. For example, if a private citizen runs a company that fails due to fraud, they could be held personally liable for repaying debts or compensating investors. Legal protections, such as bankruptcy, may help them discharge certain debts, but the financial and legal consequences can be devastating and long-lasting.

CHAPTER 4

Divergent Upbringing, Education, and Professional Background

The typical journey to becoming a federal lawmaker in the United States is shaped by a unique blend of social, educational, and professional experiences. While each individual's path differs, there are common patterns among a majority of federal lawmakers, especially in terms of their upbringing, education, and career trajectory. These factors help shape their political values, governing style, and ability to navigate the complex landscape of American politics.

Many federal lawmakers come from backgrounds that instill a strong sense of civic duty, leadership, and public service from a young age. While they represent various economic and social strata, a significant number come from upper-middle-class families that emphasize education, responsibility, and community involvement.

A significant proportion of federal lawmakers come from families with histories of public service, either in law, government, or military service. For instance, George W. Bush, the 43rd President of the United States, followed in the footsteps of his father, George H.W. Bush, who was a former president, and his grandfather, Prescott Bush, who served as a U.S. senator. This kind of familial tradition in public service can inspire an early interest in governance and provide early exposure to the privileges of political life.

Similarly, many lawmakers come from families with a strong legal background. Justice Elena Kagan, before becoming a U.S. Supreme Court Justice, served in various legal and academic roles, and she was raised in a family where intellectualism and legal discourse were deeply valued. While she is not a federal lawmaker, her pathway parallels many legislators who come from legally inclined families.

Many lawmakers grow up in relatively privileged environments, which provide them access to quality education and networks of influence. Lawmakers such as former Speaker of the House Paul Ryan came from a comfortable background, with access to good schools and early exposure to conservative principles through family and community influence.

There are some exceptions to this norm, lawmakers like Senator Tammy Duckworth, were raised in more financially unstable situations. Her family faced poverty during her teenage years, but her upbringing emphasized the value of service, as her father was a World War II veteran. This instilled a sense of duty, leading to her military service and eventual political career.

Many future lawmakers were raised in households where community engagement and activism were emphasized. For example, former President Barack Obama, though raised in an upper middle-class environment, was heavily influenced by his grandparents, who were engaged in civic activities, and his mother, who taught him to value social justice and equality. This early exposure often fosters an awareness of societal challenges and a desire to contribute to societal improvement. Education plays a pivotal role in the development of most federal lawmakers. While there is diversity in where lawmakers are educated, many attend elite universities and pursue degrees in fields that prepare them for a career in law and public policy.

A significant portion of federal lawmakers are graduates of Ivy League institutions or other prestigious universities. These institutions, such as Harvard, Yale, Princeton, and Stanford, are known for producing leaders in law, business, and politics. Many lawmakers, including notable figures like Senator Ted Cruz (Princeton and Harvard Law) and Senator Elizabeth Warren (Rutgers and Harvard Law professor), have taken this path. These schools not only provide a high-quality education but also expose students to powerful networks and prestigious internships that are instrumental in building political careers. Many lawmakers are involved in debate clubs, political science associations, or student government, which serve as early training grounds for the world of politics.

An overwhelming majority of federal lawmakers hold law degrees. Law schools are a traditional breeding ground for political leaders because they teach the skills necessary for governance: understanding legal frameworks, critical thinking, and mastering the art of argumentation. For example, both former President Bill Clinton and former Secretary of State Hillary Clinton graduated from Yale Law School. Similarly, Senator Kamala Harris, before becoming Vice President, earned her law degree from the University of California, Hastings, and served as a prosecutor before entering politics.

Having a legal education equips lawmakers with the ability to draft legislation, understand constitutional issues, and navigate the legislative process. This professional background also opens doors to clerkships with judges, work in law firms, or roles as prosecutors, all of which provide further political training. Some lawmakers come from backgrounds in public policy, economics, or business, often earning degrees in these fields. For instance, Senator Mitt Romney holds a joint MBA/JD from Harvard, blending legal and business education that paved the way for his career in both the private and public sectors. These degrees are valuable for lawmakers who focus on economic issues, budget management, or business-related legislation. Their training in managing large organizations, analyzing data, and understanding economic trends allegedly makes them well-suited to tackle complex legislative issues.

Before entering Congress, many lawmakers build careers in law, public service, business, or military service. Their professional experiences often define the issues they champion and shape their leadership style. These roles give them experience in legal interpretation, public speaking, and advocacy, all of which are vital skills in Congress.

For example, Congressman Adam Schiff, the lead impeachment manager during Donald Trump's impeachment trial, served as an assistant U.S. attorney before entering politics, honing his skills in litigation and investigation.

Historically, some lawmakers had military backgrounds, which often translate into leadership roles in defense and foreign policy. Senator John McCain, who served in the U.S. Navy was one of the examples of this pathway. His military service was central to his political career and informed his strong stance on national security issues. Similarly, Senator Tammy Duckworth, who lost both legs during her service in the Iraq War, has been a strong advocate for veterans' affairs and defense policy. Military experience often provides lawmakers with leadership training and a deep understanding of the sacrifices involved in national service. Unfortunately, few current politicians were active duty military veterans, and even fewer have ever been in combat.

Many lawmakers come from careers in public service, including work as community organizers, city council members, state legislators, or in other government roles. For instance, Congresswoman Alexandria Ocasio-Cortez began her career as an activist and organizer before being put on an election ballot to propagate leftist political issues like income inequality and climate change. Many state lawmakers use their local political experience as a steppingstone to the federal level.

A number of lawmakers, especially Republicans, come from business backgrounds. These individuals often emphasize free-market policies, economic growth, and fiscal responsibility. For example, Senator Ron Johnson of Wisconsin had a long career in manufacturing before entering politics, bringing with him a focus on deregulation and business-friendly policies. These lawmakers typically bring an understanding of economic management and budgetary oversight from their business experience, influencing how they approach legislation related to economic development and business regulations.

To their credit, the typical federal lawmaker enjoyed an upbringing that encouraged leadership and civic responsibility, an elite educational background often anchored in legal or business studies, and a professional career that builds expertise in law, public service, or business. These common experiences equip them with the skills and networks necessary to navigate the complex world of federal politics. While the specifics of their journeys vary, most federal lawmakers share these formative experiences, creating a disconnected professional class well-versed in law, governance, and public policy. But how about the rank and file citizenry? Let's compare politicians and corporate elites with community-level small business owners and private citizens.

Community-level business owners and private citizens play a vital role in the fabric of local economies, often providing essential services and fostering personal connections within neighborhoods. While an entrepreneur's path is unique, there are common trends in the upbringing, education, and professional background of these individuals, shaped by both personal drive and community involvement. Unlike large-scale business moguls, community business owners tend to be more deeply integrated into the daily lives of their customers and are often shaped by their immediate environments.

The upbringing of many community-level business owners often reflects a blend of family values, an entrepreneurial spirit, and a strong sense of community. While some may come from entrepreneurial families, others are motivated by a desire for independence or the need to improve their family's personal circumstances. Many community business owners are raised in families that already operate small businesses. This upbringing exposes them to the day-to-day realities of entrepreneurship, such as managing finances, interacting with customers, and balancing personal and professional responsibilities. For instance, a family that runs a local grocery store or diner might pass down the business through generations, providing a hands-on education to the next generation about running a business.

These family-owned businesses foster a sense of responsibility and continuity, as seen in cases like Italian family restaurants, hardware stores, or local bakeries that have been in business for decades. The children of such business owners often learn valuable skills at an early age, such as how to interact with customers or handle inventory, which later inform their own ventures.

Many community business owners come from middle-class families that emphasize the value of hard work, financial independence, and the importance of being self-sufficient. These individuals often grow up watching their parents work regular jobs and may be encouraged to start part-time jobs as teenagers. This instills a strong work ethic and a desire for control over their own financial destiny. For instance, someone raised in a middle-class home where parents are teachers, or blue-collar workers, might aspire to open their own construction company, hair salon, or coffee shop. The desire to be their own boss and create something lasting drives them to pursue entrepreneurship.

Many community-level business owners grow up in tight-knit communities where relationships are highly valued. These early experiences shape their business mindset, often resulting in a strong customer-first approach. Owners of local retail stores, florists, or auto repair shops may have grown up with a deep sense of loyalty to their neighborhoods, inspiring them to start businesses that serve local needs. This can be particularly true for immigrants or second-generation Americans who settle in communities where they seek to provide culturally specific goods or services, such as ethnic grocery stores, restaurants, or specialty shops. Their upbringing in a culturally rich, community-driven environment influences their decision to open businesses that reflect their heritage and meet the needs of their community.

While some community business owners pursue higher education, many are self-taught or gain practical knowledge through apprenticeships, trade schools, or hands-on experiences. Unlike corporate elites and politicians, community business owners often rely on practical skills more than academic credentials.

A significant number of community-level business owners come from vocational or technical educational backgrounds. Trade schools and apprenticeships provide hands-on learning, and specific skill sets that are directly applicable to small business operations. For example, electricians, plumbers, or auto mechanics, and other people who make the lifestyles of the elite possible, often attend vocational schools and later open their own service-oriented businesses.. A plumber who starts his own plumbing business or a beautician who opens her own salon is likely to have gained technical skills through a combination of trade school education and apprenticeship with an experienced professional. These types of business owners often build their careers on the specialized skills they learned and perfected over years of practice.

Some community business owners have only a high school education but compensate with a strong work ethic, a keen understanding of their local market, and self-taught business skills. For instance, owners of landscaping businesses, local restaurants, or cleaning services may not have formal business training but learn the ropes by starting small, working within their communities, and gaining experience over time. Self-taught business owners often take the initiative to learn essential business skills, such as bookkeeping, marketing, and customer relations, through online resources, mentorship, or trial and error. They might start a side hustle or gig that evolves into a full-time business after learning the basics of managing a small operation.

While many community-level business owners rely on practical skills, some have formal educational backgrounds in business or related fields. A small number of entrepreneurs pursue business degrees at community colleges or universities, learning the fundamentals of accounting, marketing, and management. These individuals may apply their academic training to local businesses such as retail stores, cafés, or fitness centers. For example, a person who earned a business degree might decide to open a local coffee shop or boutique, using their education to handle business planning, financial management, and marketing strategies. They might apply lessons from school, like conducting market research or managing cash flow, to ensure the success of their business thereby contributing to their communities.

Unlike lawmakers and political elites, community business owners are deeply embedded in the lives of their communities, offering essential goods and services while contributing to the overall well-being of their neighborhoods. Their path to entrepreneurship exemplifies the diversity and resilience of small business owners across the country.

What About Regular People?

The life journey of a typical non-business owning private citizen in the United States is also shaped by factors that blend upbringing, educational background, and professional experiences. While the specifics of each individual's path vary widely, common trends emerge that reflect societal norms, access to education, and the nature of work in the modern economy. Unlike entrepreneurs, these individuals tend to follow more conventional career paths, often finding stable employment in established organizations rather than pursuing independent business ventures.

The upbringing of most private citizens is influenced by family dynamics, socio-economic status, and cultural values. These factors shape their outlook on work, education, and life goals. A strong emphasis is often placed on personal responsibility, finding steady employment, and achieving a work-life balance. A large number of citizens come from middle-class families, which emphasize stability, education, and practical career choices. These individuals often grow up in stable households where parents work typical 7-to-5 jobs and prioritize steady income over entrepreneurial risks. Their upbringing reflects a focus on security and a comfortable lifestyle. For example, a child raised in a suburban environment with parents who work as teachers, nurses, or office workers often learns the value of stable employment and the importance of maintaining a balanced family life. The stability of the middle class often fosters expectations of a similar path, such as attending college and securing a traditional job.

People from working-class backgrounds are often raised in environments where hard work and practical job skills are emphasized over formal education. These individuals may be exposed to blue-collar work through their parents or community members and are taught the value of physical labor and reliability. For instance, a person growing up in a rural or industrial area where parents work as factory laborers, mechanics, or construction workers might be encouraged to find employment in similar trades. The emphasis is typically on securing a reliable job that provides benefits and income to support a family, rather than taking the risks associated with entrepreneurship.

For most private citizens, education also serves as the foundation for achieving stability and success. While there are a variety of educational pathways, many people pursue traditional forms of higher education or vocational training, depending on their personal circumstances and career goals. While higher education is common, many people do not pursue college degrees. Some enter the workforce directly after high school, finding employment in retail, manufacturing, or the service industry. For these individuals, the focus is often on gaining practical job experience and gradually building a career through hard work and on-the-job training. Whether working in the public or private sector, these individuals often value job security, benefits, and a balanced work-life dynamic, contributing meaningfully to society without the need for government to run their lives.

CHAPTER 5

Lawmakers Disconnected from Constituent Challenges

Lawmakers and political elites often make decisions based on what they believe is best for society as a whole, operating within a framework of public policy, economics, and governance. They typically view themselves as stewards of the public good, charged with addressing broad societal challenges such as economic inequality, public health, national security, and environmental sustainability. Their decisions are often informed by data, expert testimony, political ideologies, and long-term strategic goals. However, this top-down approach to decision-making can sometimes feel disconnected from the everyday struggles of individuals, particularly those in small communities or businesses, who navigate challenges more intimately and personally.

In contrast, community-based business owners and private citizens make decisions rooted in personal experience, experience that includes managing the daily pressures of running a business, supporting a family, and coping with the economic conditions that lawmakers themselves help to shape. These individuals tend to prioritize immediate, practical concerns, making choices that directly impact their livelihood, their employees, and their families.

Lawmakers and political elites are often removed from the immediate effects of the policies they enact. Their decisions are frequently based on abstract principles, macroeconomic trends, or ideological frameworks. For example, during economic crises, they might implement austerity measures or increase taxes, believing these policies are necessary to stabilize the national economy or balance budgets. From their disconnected perspective, these choices are intended to promote long-term prosperity or sustainability for the country.

Similarly, policies related to public health, such as pandemic restrictions or environmental regulations, are often seen as measures to protect the public good, based on "expert" recommendations and global trends.

For instance, during the COVID-19 pandemic, many lawmakers and political elites worldwide implemented lockdowns, mask mandates, and vaccination campaigns in an effort to curb the spread of the virus and prevent overwhelming healthcare systems. These decisions were allegedly informed by scientific data and public health models, but they often failed to consider the nuanced, day-to-day realities faced by business owners and workers. For example, small business owners in industries like hospitality, retail, or personal services faced the closure of their businesses and layoffs of employees, resulting in immediate financial distress. While lawmakers may have seen these decisions as essential for public safety, the ripple effects on local economies and individual livelihoods were profound.

Lawmakers also approach issues like climate change from a high-level perspective, implementing carbon taxes or environmental regulations intended to reduce emissions and promote sustainability. While the goal may be to protect future generations from environmental degradation, the short-term impact on small businesses or individuals, such as increased energy costs or new regulatory burdens, can be harsh, especially for those who have limited resources to adapt.

In many cases, lawmakers and political elites rely on technocratic solutions or broad strokes policy tools, which they believe will solve societal problems but may unintentionally create additional hardships for communities they don't directly experience. Their decisions are often driven by theoretical knowledge, academic research, and sometimes even political interests, which can make their understanding of the everyday lives of citizens feel abstract or distant.

In contrast, community-based business owners and other private citizens make decisions that are grounded in personal, lived experience. They navigate the intersection of family, finances, and community every day, making decisions based on the immediate needs and challenges they face. Small business owners, in particular, are intimately familiar with the struggles of maintaining a business in a fluctuating economy, dealing with taxes, managing regulations, and ensuring the well-being of their employees and customers. Their decisions are inherently practical, shaped by their proximity to the consequences of both economic and family pressures.

For example, a local restaurant owner may decide to close for a few weeks to remodel in order to attract more customers, even though it may strain cash flow. This decision is based on their understanding of the local market, personal financial situation, and what their family can afford to sacrifice in the short term for long-term stability. Their approach to challenges is pragmatic. They can see, feel, and experience the consequences of each decision they make in real time.

These individuals also make choices based on navigating challenges imposed by lawmakers. For instance, a small business owner facing new tax hikes or regulatory burdens may have to make difficult decisions about raising prices, reducing staff, or cutting costs in other areas. While lawmakers might see these policies as necessary for the broader public good, the small business owner feels the direct impact on their ability to sustain their business and keep people employed. Similarly, a family dealing with rising healthcare costs, new zoning laws, or education reforms must weigh how these policies will affect their children, their mortgage payments, and their day-to-day life.

Community-based decision-making is highly adaptive, often driven by a combination of personal intuition, experience, and the needs of those around them. A small construction company might take on extra hours or diversify into new service areas because they see demand rising locally or because they need to provide for their employees' families, who are also part of the local community. These decisions are more immediate, focused on survival and growth within a constrained environment. Unlike political elites, who operate from a top-down viewpoint, local business owners and private citizens make decisions based on what directly affects them, their family members, and their employees in the short term.

Lawmakers Disconnected from Local Challenges

While lawmakers may craft policies with the intention of helping the economy or society at large, the impact on local business owners and citizens can often feel disconnected from the real-world challenges they face. For example, a lawmaker pushing for higher corporate taxes or increased regulations on emissions may not fully understand the impact on a small trucking company that already operates on slim margins. The same goes for tax policies that may be beneficial for the national economy but could force a local entrepreneur to delay hiring or expansion plans, directly affecting job creation in a community.

Similarly, education reform laws designed to improve overall academic outcomes might overlook the unique needs of families in rural areas who lack access to the technology required for new virtual learning mandates. Or consider healthcare mandates that increase coverage requirements for small businesses. While the intention may be to provide better benefits for employees, the immediate effect might be that small businesses struggle to afford premiums, forcing them to reduce hours or cut jobs altogether.

The motivations behind decisions made by lawmakers and political elites versus community business owners reflect different realities. Political elites often make decisions based on national or even global objectives, often without directly experiencing the consequences of those decisions in their personal lives. They are typically more insulated from the immediate impact of economic recessions, regulatory burdens, or public health mandates. While they may have broad knowledge of economic trends or long-term societal needs, their decisions are often detached from the everyday experiences of most citizens.

Consequently, community-based business owners and private citizens live with the outcomes of those decisions. Their choices are shaped by the immediate realities of balancing family budgets, keeping businesses open, managing local labor markets, and adapting to changing government policies. They must deal with the direct consequences of laws passed in distant capitals, and they do so with an understanding rooted in their own experience of economic and family struggles.

For example, a family-owned grocery store in a small town may have to adjust pricing, payroll, and inventory to cope with inflation and supply chain disruptions that stem from government policies or global crises. The lawmakers who crafted policies contributing to those disruptions might have acted with the belief that they were doing what was best for the economy or public health, but the community-based business owner feels the effects acutely and personally.

In essence, the decisions made by lawmakers and political elites revolve around abstract goals and ideological beliefs about what is best for society at large, often removed from the on-the-ground realities faced by local business owners and private citizens. Community-based decision-makers, on the other hand, must constantly adapt to both personal and external pressures, including those imposed by lawmakers. Their choices are grounded in lived experience, personal sacrifice, and the need to navigate immediate family and economic challenges. This fundamental difference between top-down governance and ground-level decision-making highlights the contrast between policy creation and its real-world impact, a tension that often defines the relationship between government and everyday citizens.

CHAPTER 6

The Disconnect Between Politicians and Lawmakers, and We the Public

The phrase "we are in this together" has been widely used by political leaders, public figures, and institutions during moments of crisis or significant societal challenges to evoke a sense of unity, shared responsibility, and collective action. Below is a narrative outlining several notable occasions and contexts in which this phrase has been used, along with the figures and organizations that employed it.

The global financial crisis of 2008 led to widespread economic upheaval, with banks failing, stock markets crashing, and millions losing their homes and jobs. During this period, political leaders used the phrase "we are in this together" to reassure citizens that governments and financial institutions were working together to address the crisis and stabilize economies.

President Barack Obama frequently used variations of the phrase during his speeches on the economy, emphasizing that all Americans, regardless of their socio-economic background, would need to make sacrifices to rebuild the economy. Like Vladimer Lenin, Obama framed the recovery efforts as a shared national endeavor, despite the fact that the financial sector, which largely caused the crisis, received massive bailouts while millions of Americans suffered.

Perhaps the most prominent and frequent use of the phrase "we are in this together" occurred during the COVID-19 pandemic. As the virus spread globally, governments, public health authorities, and global organizations sought to convey solidarity in the face of an unprecedented health crisis. World Health Organization leaders, including Director-General Tedros Adhanom Ghebreyesus, used the phrase in their global appeals for cooperation, stressing the importance of international collaboration to combat the virus. The message was allegedly meant to emphasize that no country, regardless of wealth or power, was immune from the virus's impacts.

Political leaders such as British Prime Minister Boris Johnson and Canadian Prime Minister Justin Trudeau echoed this sentiment. Johnson, who himself contracted COVID-19, used the phrase during national addresses to the U.K., urging citizens to comply with lockdowns and health measures. Trudeau similarly framed his government's response as a collective effort, asking Canadians to endure economic and social sacrifices for the greater good.

In the U.S., President Joe Biden frequently used the phrase as part of his administration's messaging on the pandemic, particularly around vaccination efforts and the economic recovery. He stressed that beating the virus and rebuilding the economy would require collective action and unity.

The phrase "we are in this together" has been used by environmental advocates and political leaders to discuss climate change, positioning it as a global challenge requiring coordinated international action.

The World Economic Forum, led by Klaus Schwab, has invoked the phrase in discussions around global sustainability efforts. The WEF's Great Reset initiative, which calls for rethinking global capitalism in the wake of the pandemic, often emphasizes that addressing climate change and rebuilding economies must involve cooperation across governments, businesses, and civil society.

U.S. climate envoy John Kerry used similar language when addressing international forums, arguing that climate change knows no borders and requires collective action to mitigate its impacts. The phrase was often used to stress that even though the consequences of climate change disproportionately affect poorer nations and communities, all countries must work together to solve the crisis.

The summer of 2020 saw massive protests following the killing of convicted drug dealer George Floyd and the broader reckoning with racial injustice in the United States and around the world. Politicians and corporate leaders used "we are in this together" to communicate solidarity with social justice movements.

Corporations such as Nike, Apple, and Google adopted the phrase in their public statements and advertising campaigns, signaling their support for racial justice and their purported commitment to diversity and inclusion. While critics argued that many of these companies benefited from systemic inequalities, the message was aimed at showing unity with those calling for societal change.

Politicians such as New York Governor Andrew Cuomo used variations of the phrase during press briefings, particularly when addressing the overlap of the COVID-19 pandemic with racial disparities. He framed the fight against the virus and against systemic racism as interconnected challenges that required collective empathy and action.

"We are in this together" has been invoked in discussions of economic inequality, particularly in response to policies that aim to address wealth gaps and social safety nets.

Senator Bernie Sanders has often used the phrase or similar language during his campaigns and speeches advocating for universal healthcare, living wages, and social welfare programs. He frames these issues as ones that affect the broader population, particularly the working class and middle class, who must unite to demand change from the political and economic elite.

During debates over the expansion of unemployment benefits, President Biden and House Speaker Nancy Pelosi invoked the phrase to argue that government relief during the pandemic was necessary for all Americans to recover from economic fallout. They emphasized that a collective effort was needed to lift everyone out of the recession caused by COVID-19.

Global organizations often use "we are in this together" when discussing global governance challenges that transcend national borders, such as migration, poverty, and international conflicts.

The United Nations frequently invokes the phrase in its humanitarian appeals and during international summits, particularly those related to the Sustainable Development Goals. The message is meant to foster international solidarity around global poverty, health, education, and environmental challenges.

The European Union, especially in the aftermath of the Brexit vote, has emphasized the need for unity among member states, using language akin to "we are in this together" to underscore that the benefits of cooperation outweigh the challenges of fragmentation.

In moments of economic uncertainty, such as during recessions or the aftermath of market crashes, political leaders have often used the phrase to convey a sense of national unity and shared responsibility.

During the 2008 financial crisis, then-President George W. Bush and subsequently President Barack Obama used the phrase to stress that all Americans, from Wall Street to Main Street, would need to make sacrifices to help the economy recover. However, many critics pointed out that the government's bailouts favored large corporations and financial institutions, while the average American faced foreclosures and job losses, raising questions about whether "we" were truly in it together.

A Closer Look

The phrase "we are in this together" has been used repeatedly by political leaders, corporations, and global institutions to foster a sense of unity and shared responsibility during times of crisis, whether in response to economic challenges, public health emergencies, or social justice movements. However, the rhetoric has often been met with skepticism, as critics argue that the burdens of these crises are not shared equally. While the phrase aims to communicate solidarity, in practice, the wealthy and powerful often avoid the harshest consequences, leaving ordinary citizens to bear the brunt of the sacrifices. The use of this phrase, therefore, reflects both a genuine call for unity and a broader disconnect between elites and the populations they claim to represent.

The title of this book, "We Are NOT in This Together" takes on profound meaning when examining the Social Security system in the United States, particularly the decisions made by lawmakers and political elites to cap Federal Insurance Contributions Act (FICA) taxes, a policy that disproportionately benefits top wage earners while placing a heavier burden on average citizens. Despite claims that everyone contributes fairly to Social Security, in practice, the structure of FICA taxes reveals deep inequalities in how the system is funded and who truly bears the cost.

The FICA Tax Cap

Under current U.S. law, only the first portion of an individual's earnings is subject to Social Security taxes. As of 2024, income above $160,200 is exempt from the 6.2% Social Security tax that all wage earners pay. This is known as the FICA tax cap, and it means that high-income earners do not pay Social Security taxes on any income they earn beyond this threshold. This policy disproportionately benefits the wealthy, who may earn millions but only pay into the Social Security system on a fraction of their total income.

For example, a worker earning $160,200 will pay the same amount in Social Security taxes as a CEO earning $10 million a year. This creates a significant disparity in how much different income groups contribute to the Social Security system. While lower and middle-class workers pay 6.2% of their income up to the cap, high earners effectively pay a much smaller percentage of their total income. In other words, the higher someone's earnings are above the cap, the less they contribute, relative to their income.

What makes this situation even more striking is that despite paying proportionally less into the system, high-income earners are still entitled to draw from the Social Security fund upon retirement, just like everyone else. This means that while the cap shields their higher earnings from taxation, they can still receive benefits based on their lifetime contributions up to the cap. In essence, top wage earners benefit from a system they contribute less to than those who earn significantly less.

This structural inequity illustrates a stark contrast between the rhetoric of "shared sacrifice" often promoted by political elites and the reality of how the Social Security system is funded. The burden of funding Social Security falls disproportionately on the middle class, while the wealthiest Americans are insulated from paying their fair share. Yet, when these wealthy individuals retire, they will still draw from the same fund as lower-income workers who contributed a higher percentage of their wages over their lifetimes.

Over the years, legislation designed to "strengthen" Social Security has often done so at the expense of benefit recipients, without addressing the underlying inequities in how the system is funded. In particular, past benefit reduction measures have increased the financial strain on average Social Security recipients, without imposing additional costs on high earners or large corporations.

For example, in 1983, Congress passed the Social Security Amendments, which raised the full retirement age from 65 to 67. This shift was designed to reduce the long-term costs of Social Security by delaying when people could begin receiving full benefits. However, this policy disproportionately affected lower-income workers, who often rely on Social Security as their primary source of retirement income. Many lower-income workers, particularly those in physically demanding jobs, are unable to work into their late 60s, and therefore they are forced to retire early and receive permanently reduced benefits.

In contrast, wealthy individuals, who are less likely to rely on Social Security as their primary source of income, were largely unaffected by this change. These individuals often have other forms of retirement savings, such as 401(k) plans, pensions, or investments, and are more likely to be able to continue working into their 60s or beyond if they choose. The burden of reduced Social Security benefits, therefore, falls most heavily on those who have the least financial flexibility.

Another example of benefit reduction legislation is the Social Security tax increase of 1983, which raised the payroll tax rate to build up a surplus in the Social Security trust fund. While this measure was intended to shore up the system's finances, it also increased the financial burden on workers, particularly those earning less than the FICA cap. The wealthy, again, were largely shielded from this increase due to the cap on taxable earnings.

The Disconnect Between Lawmakers and the Public

The decision to maintain the FICA tax cap, while simultaneously passing legislation that reduces benefits or increases taxes on average workers, underscores the disconnect between lawmakers and the general public. Political elites, many of whom are part of the top wage-earning bracket, have a vested interest in maintaining the cap because it protects their own wealth from additional taxation. Yet, they are able to continue drawing Social Security benefits upon retirement, even though their proportional contribution to the system is far smaller than that of average workers.

This dynamic is compounded by the fact that many political elites and lawmakers are often wealthy enough to have significant retirement savings outside of Social Security. As a result, they are less dependent on the system and less personally affected by changes that reduce benefits or increase taxes. For the average worker, however, Social Security is a critical lifeline in retirement, and even modest reductions in benefits can have a significant impact on their financial security.

We Are Definitely Not in This Together

The phrase "we are in this together" is often used by political elites to promote policies that ask for shared sacrifice in times of economic crises, recessions, or major social changes. However, when it comes to Social Security, it is clear that we are not, in fact, all sharing the same burden. While lawmakers and top wage earners are insulated from the full effects of Social Security taxes and benefit reductions, average workers—especially those in low- and middle-income brackets, bear the brunt of these policies.

The FICA tax cap is a clear example of how the system is structured to benefit the wealthy at the expense of ordinary workers. The burden of funding Social Security is shouldered by those who can least afford it, while the wealthiest Americans contribute only a small fraction of their total income and still receive the same benefits. Meanwhile, legislative efforts to reduce the costs of Social Security often target benefit reductions or tax increases on average workers, further deepening the inequality.

The Social Security system, while critical to the financial well-being of millions of Americans, is an example of how policies crafted by political elites often disproportionately burden the middle class and the poor while allowing the wealthy to avoid their fair share. The decision to cap FICA taxes, while still allowing high earners to draw benefits from the system, creates a two-tiered system of contributions.

Meanwhile, past benefit reduction legislation has shifted more of the financial burden onto those who rely most on Social Security, further illustrating the divide between the rhetoric of "shared sacrifice" and the reality of how policies are implemented. As lawmakers continue to grapple with Social Security's future, it is clear that we are NOT all "in this together" when it comes to funding and benefiting from the system.

Another powerful example of how lawmakers and political elites assume the right to mandate and regulate how private citizens live, while largely insulating themselves from the consequences of their own legislation, can be seen in the Affordable Care Act (ACA), also known as "Obamacare." This sweeping health care reform, passed in 2010, was designed to make healthcare more accessible and affordable for millions of Americans. However, while the ACA placed significant financial and personal obligations on private citizens, lawmakers and political elites were often exempt from the burdens and restrictions that they imposed on the general population.

One of the central features of the ACA was the individual mandate, which required all Americans to obtain health insurance or face a financial penalty. This mandate was intended to ensure that everyone contributed to the health insurance system, thus lowering costs overall by increasing the number of insured individuals. While well-intentioned, this mandate placed a significant financial burden on millions of Americans, particularly those in the middle class who were not poor enough to qualify for Medicaid but could not easily afford the rising premiums of private health insurance.

Many citizens found themselves in a difficult position. They either had to purchase expensive health insurance that they may not have been able to afford, or they faced penalties at tax time. For families struggling to make ends meet, this mandate added another layer of financial strain. Though subsidies were available to some, the costs of compliance with the ACA were substantial for many.

Lawmaker Exemptions from the ACA

In contrast to private citizens, members of Congress and many political elites were initially exempt from the ACA's provisions. Prior to the law's implementation, lawmakers and their staff were covered under the Federal Employees Health Benefits Program (FEHBP), a high-quality health insurance plan subsidized by the government. Even after the ACA was passed, many lawmakers continued to receive subsidized health insurance that shielded them from the same financial pressures imposed on average Americans. In fact, it was only due to public outcry that Congress was eventually required to purchase health insurance through the ACA's exchanges, yet they still received generous subsidies to cover the costs.

This highlights yet another fundamental divide between lawmakers and the public. While ordinary Americans were subject to the penalties, rising premiums, and limited options under the ACA, members of

Congress were able to avoid many of these burdens through government-subsidized coverage. Additionally, political elites were largely insulated from the long-term consequences of the ACA's success or failure because they had access to better healthcare options that the average citizen could not.

Lack of Accountability for Lawmakers

Moreover, the ACA is just one example of how lawmakers are often able to create and enforce laws that regulate the lives of private citizens while remaining largely unaccountable for those laws' consequences. While average Americans faced real-world impacts, like increased premiums, higher out-of-pocket costs, and difficulties navigating the healthcare exchanges, lawmakers who crafted and passed the ACA were able to avoid many of these hardships.

Furthermore, while in office, members of Congress are largely immune from legal repercussions related to their legislative actions due to protections like the Speech or Debate Clause of the U.S. Constitution. This clause provides immunity to lawmakers from being held legally accountable for actions taken as part of their legislative duties. Essentially, lawmakers can pass laws that dramatically affect the lives of millions of Americans without bearing personal responsibility for the outcomes, at least while they are in office. The accountability mechanisms that hold private citizens to the letter of the law, such as fines, penalties, and legal challenges, rarely apply to lawmakers in the same way.

The Disconnect Between Lawmakers and the Public

This dynamic underscores a broader trend. Lawmakers and political elites frequently legislate based on what they believe is best for others, often detached from the lived experiences of the people their laws impact. The consequences and costs of these decisions, whether in healthcare, taxes, or social policy, are borne by the public, while lawmakers themselves remain shielded from many of the negative effects.

The examples of the FICA cap and the Affordable Care Act highlight a broader issue in American governance. lawmakers and political elites often impose laws and regulations that govern the lives of private citizens, all while bearing little accountability for the consequences of those laws on themselves. Whether through exemptions, subsidies, or legal protections, political elites frequently shield themselves from the impacts of the policies they create. This disconnect reveals an oligarchical government, where those in power mandate how the public should live yet, manage to avoid being bound by the same constraints, all while declaring that such measures are in the best interest of everyone.

CHAPTER 7

Elitists Feigned Attempts to Relate

Historically, many legislative proposals aimed at "leveling the economic playing field" have included increased taxes and regulations imposed on private citizens, especially the middle class, while often exempting lawmakers and the powerful benefactors of these policies, corporate elites, wealthy donors, and special interest groups. These proposals have, in effect, created policies that appear to promote equality but instead leave the economic burden on ordinary citizens. Meanwhile, lawmakers and those benefiting from these policies face fewer consequences or manage to escape significant financial responsibility. Here's a detailed exploration of how these dynamics have unfolded:

The Progressive Income Tax

One of the most common tools for leveling the economic playing field is the progressive income tax system, which is designed to tax higher incomes at higher rates. While this may seem fair in principle, the reality of how tax policies have been implemented shows that working-class citizens often bear a disproportionate share of the tax burden compared to the wealthy elite.

In the 1980s and 1990s, lawmakers proposed tax reforms that were ostensibly aimed at the wealthy. However, these reforms often resulted in tax cuts for corporations and top earners, while expanding loopholes for the wealthy through capital gains taxes, real estate deductions, and offshore accounts. Meanwhile, taxes on wages remained high for ordinary workers. For example, while Ronald Reagan's 1981 Economic Recovery Tax Act slashed the top marginal tax rate from 70% to 50%, the middle class faced higher payroll taxes as a result of increases in Social Security and Medicare taxes.

The Tax Reform Act of 1986, championed by Reagan, was supposed to simplify the tax code and eliminate tax shelters for the wealthy. While it succeeded in closing some loopholes, it also removed many deductions that middle-class citizens had previously relied on. The effective tax burden on wage earners did not ease as significantly as it did for corporations and wealthier individuals, who continued to benefit from new tax strategies and financial engineering.

Despite calls for higher taxes on the wealthy, lawmakers themselves often benefit from policies that protect their income and wealth. Congressional members have the ability to influence tax legislation that preserves their wealth, such as tax shelters and deductions for real estate investments, capital gains, and inherited wealth. The real estate loopholes, for example, continue to allow the wealthiest to shelter income while lawmakers rarely target this asset class, as many of them invest heavily in real estate themselves.

Efforts to tax corporations more aggressively or to introduce regulatory frameworks that ensure businesses pay their fair share have frequently resulted in increased costs for consumers and small businesses, rather than the intended large corporations. This is often because large corporations, with their powerful lobbying arms, manage to negotiate exemptions or find ways to shift the financial burden onto their customers or smaller competitors.

The Corporate Tax Cuts and Jobs Act (2017)

The Tax Cuts and Jobs Act (TCJA) of 2017 is a prime example of this dynamic. While the bill was marketed as a way to make U.S. corporations more competitive by cutting the corporate tax rate from 35% to 21%, it was also touted as a way to boost middle-class prosperity through job creation and wage growth.

In reality large corporations used the bulk of their tax savings not to hire more workers or raise wages, but to engage in stock buybacks that enriched their executives and shareholders. Ordinary workers saw only modest, short-term benefits, such as one-time bonuses (taxed as income), while the long-term cost of these tax cuts added significantly to the federal deficit, creating pressure to cut social programs that disproportionately benefit the middle and working class.

At the same time, corporate lobbying efforts ensured that many major corporations could still use loopholes to pay little to no federal taxes. In 2018, despite the new lower corporate tax rate, companies like Amazon and Netflix paid zero federal taxes. Meanwhile, small businesses and private citizens continued to shoulder a heavier tax burden relative to their income.

Lawmakers often protect their own financial interests through investments in these same corporations. As some of the wealthiest members of Congress hold significant stock portfolios, they directly benefit from corporate tax cuts and stock buybacks. This creates a conflict of interest where they may push for legislation that favors large businesses, with full knowledge it will benefit them personally. This dynamic is especially problematic when considering how insider trading scandals have implicated members of Congress who trade stocks based on non-public information gained through their legislative work.

Healthcare Reforms

Healthcare reform is another area where policies proposed to "level the playing field" often disproportionately affect private citizens, while lawmakers and the wealthy benefit from exemptions or more favorable alternatives. It was discussed earlier but bears repeating here.

The Affordable Care Act (ACA), passed in 2010, was meant to expand healthcare coverage and reduce costs. While the ACA did increase access to healthcare for millions of Americans, it also created new challenges for the middle class, particularly with higher premiums. Middle-class citizens who did not qualify for subsidies faced significant increases in their health insurance premiums. Many small business owners and self-employed individuals found their healthcare costs rising dramatically as insurance companies adjusted their pricing models to comply with the ACA's regulations. Before the individual mandate was repealed in 2019, individuals who did not obtain health insurance were subject to a tax penalty, placing an additional financial burden on private citizens.

While the general population grappled with rising healthcare costs and insurance mandates, members of Congress enjoyed premium healthcare plans through the Federal Employees Health Benefits Program (FEHBP). Lawmakers and their families had access to a range of high-quality insurance plans subsidized by the government. This disparity highlighted the disconnect between the healthcare burdens experienced by private citizens and the privileges enjoyed by those in power.

Environmental Regulations

Environmental legislation, especially in the context of climate change, has often been framed as essential for leveling the playing field by creating a cleaner, more sustainable world for future generations. However, the cost of these regulations frequently falls disproportionately on middle and lower income individuals.

Policies aimed at reducing carbon emissions, such as carbon taxes or renewable energy mandates, often come with significant upfront costs. These policies are supposed to incentivize corporations to adopt greener practices, but in practice, energy companies often pass the costs of compliance down to consumers through higher utility bills. In states with aggressive environmental mandates, like California, energy prices have risen, placing a heavier burden on working-class families who are less able to absorb these increased costs.

Meanwhile, corporate polluters often face less direct financial consequences for their environmental impact. Through extensive lobbying, they can negotiate favorable regulatory frameworks or access to subsidies that allow them to transition to green energy at a lower cost. Additionally, large corporations benefit from carbon credits and other market-based mechanisms that allow them to continue polluting while offsetting their emissions through financial instruments.

While ordinary citizens face higher energy costs and compliance burdens, many political elites invest heavily in the same industries benefiting from government subsidies for green technologies. In fact, federal lawmakers often hold investments in energy companies and green energy initiatives, further highlighting the disparity between the burdens on private citizens and the financial gains of those in power. We are NOT in this together.

When lawmakers propose policies to "level the playing field," the rhetoric of fairness and equality often falls flat in practice. Ordinary citizens, especially middle and working-class individuals, bear the financial and regulatory burden of these proposals, while lawmakers and the wealthy elite are frequently shielded from the consequences or benefit from exemptions. Whether through tax policies, healthcare reforms, corporate regulation, or environmental legislation, the pattern is clear: private citizens face higher costs and tighter regulations, while the economic and political elite continue to amass wealth and influence, often avoiding the very accountability they impose on the rest of society.

CHAPTER 8

One Realistic Way for Political and Corporate Elites to Be "in This" With Us

Social Security is primarily funded through payroll taxes, known as the Federal Insurance Contributions Act (FICA) tax. Currently, both employers and employees contribute 6.2% each of an employee's wages up to a cap of $160,200 (as of 2023). Self-employed individuals pay the full 12.4%. Additionally, Social Security receives revenue from taxation on benefits for higher-income recipients.

The Social Security trust fund receives roughly $1.118 trillion annually in revenue, primarily from payroll taxes (FICA) and income taxes on benefits. Here's how the key components break down:

FICA contributions: Approximately $1 trillion comes from FICA taxes, which make up the largest share of Social Security's funding. The majority of this revenue comes from workers' wages up to the capped limit of $160,200.

Income taxes on benefits: Social Security beneficiaries who have substantial incomes also pay federal income taxes on their benefits. This generates roughly $36.5 billion annually.

In 2023, Social Security paid out $1.275 trillion in benefits to around 67 million beneficiaries, including retirees, disabled workers, and survivors of deceased workers. Retirement benefits account for the largest share, distributed to approximately 49 million retirees and their dependents. Disability benefits are paid to around 9 million disabled workers and their families. Survivor benefits are distributed to 6 million survivors of deceased workers.

The Social Security Trustees Report for 2023 projects that, under the current system, the Social Security trust fund will become insolvent by 2034 if no changes are made. This means that, starting in 2034, the trust fund will no longer have sufficient reserves to pay full benefits, and beneficiaries would face an automatic reduction of about 23% in their monthly benefits unless new revenue is introduced to shore up the program.

As previously stated, the current FICA tax is only applied to wages up to $160,200, meaning any income earned beyond that limit is not subject to Social Security taxes. This cap creates a situation where high-income earners pay a smaller percentage of their overall income into Social Security compared to lower- and middle-income workers, whose entire income is taxed.

For instance, someone earning $160,200 pays FICA on their full income, while someone earning $500,000 only pays FICA on the first $160,200, leaving over two-thirds of their income untaxed for Social Security purposes. This significantly reduces the revenue potential for the Social Security program.

If the FICA cap were eliminated, all wages would be subject to the Social Security tax, which would dramatically increase the revenue flowing into the Social Security trust fund. According to recent analyses, eliminating the cap on taxable income would generate an estimated $150 billion to $200 billion annually in additional revenue. This influx of funds could extend the solvency of the Social Security trust fund by several decades.

High-income individuals earning beyond the current cap would now pay the 6.2% Social Security tax on all earnings, which would increase their contribution substantially. For example, a person earning $500,000 would pay FICA on all $500,000, not just the first $160,200, resulting in a significantly larger tax bill.

Currently, about 40% of Social Security beneficiaries pay federal income taxes on a portion of their benefits if their total income exceeds certain thresholds. Individual filers with combined income over $25,000, and married couples with combined income over $32,000. For those who do pay, up to 85% of their benefits can be taxed depending on their total income. This taxation generates about $36.5 billion annually for the Social Security trust fund.

If taxation on benefits were eliminated, that annual $36.5 billion revenue stream would be lost. However, if the FICA cap were completely removed, Social Security would collect significantly more from high-income earners, bringing in an estimated $150 billion to $200 billion more per year. This additional revenue would extend the solvency of the Social Security trust fund well beyond 2034. Depending on other factors like economic growth and demographic changes, experts estimate that eliminating the cap could extend the program's solvency into the 2070s or beyond.

To reiterate, if both the FICA cap were eliminated and taxes on Social Security benefits were repealed, Social Security could experience a net increase in revenue, even with the removal of taxes on benefits. The additional revenue from removing the cap, around $150-200 billion per year, would more than compensate for the $36.5 billion in lost revenue from taxes on benefits.

This combined approach would allow Social Security to maintain solvency for decades, potentially avoiding benefit cuts for future generations of retirees, disabled workers, and survivors. The program could continue to meet its full obligations without the ever-looming threat of insolvency.

Bibliography

Social Security Trustees Report (2023). "The 2023 Annual Report of the Board of Trustees of the Federal Old-Age and Survivors Insurance and Federal Disability Insurance Trust Funds." U.S. Social Security Administration, 2023. https://www.ssa.gov/oact/trsum/.

Tax Cuts and Jobs Act (2017). "Public Law 115-97: An Act to Provide for Reconciliation Pursuant to Titles II and V of the Concurrent Resolution on the Budget for Fiscal Year 2018." 115th Congress of the United States of America, 2017. https://www.congress.gov/115/plaws/publ97/PLAW-115publ97.pdf.

Tax Policy Center. "Distributional Analysis of the Tax Cuts and Jobs Act." Urban-Brookings Tax Policy Center, December 2017. https://www.taxpolicycenter.org/publications/distributional-analysis-tax-cuts-and-jobs-act/full.

Affordable Care Act (ACA). "Patient Protection and Affordable Care Act." Public Law 111-148, 111th Congress of the United States of America, 2010. https://www.congress.gov/111/plaws/publ148/PLAW-111publ148.pdf.

Congressional Research Service. "The Federal Employees Health Benefits Program (FEHBP): Available Health Insurance Plans for Members of Congress." Library of Congress, 2023. https://www.everycrsreport.com/reports/R43194.html.

Economic Recovery Tax Act of 1981. "Public Law 97-34." 97th Congress of the United States of America, 1981. https://www.congress.gov/bill/97th-congress/house-bill/4242.

Gilens, Martin, and Benjamin I. Page. "Testing Theories of American Politics: Elites, Interest Groups, and Average Citizens." Perspectives on Politics, vol. 12, no. 3, September 2014, pp. 564-581. Cambridge University Press, https://doi.org/10.1017/S1537592714001595.

National Academy of Social Insurance. "Options to Strengthen Social Security: Eliminating the Payroll Tax Cap." National Academy of Social Insurance, 2021. https://www.nasi.org/research/2021/eliminating-payroll-tax-cap/.

Internal Revenue Service (IRS). "Federal Insurance Contributions Act (FICA) Tax." Internal Revenue Service, 2023. https://www.irs.gov/taxtopics/tc751.

U.S. Department of the Treasury. "Revenue from Taxes on Social Security Benefits." U.S. Treasury Department, 2023. https://home.treasury.gov/data/finances-federal-government.

Urban Institute. "How Much Would Social Security Solvency Improve if the Cap on Payroll Taxes Were Raised?" Urban Institute, 2021. https://www.urban.org/policy-centers/cross-center-initiatives/program-retirement-policy/projects/data-query-how-much-would-social-security-solvency-improve-if-cap-payroll-taxes-were-raised.

www.ingramcontent.com/pod-product-compliance
Lightning Source LLC
LaVergne TN
LVHW090129160826
845673LV00015B/1129

* 9 7 9 8 2 3 0 2 8 7 0 0 1 *